Published by Ottenheimer Publishers, Inc.
Distributed by Rand McNally & Company.
Printed in Hong Kong.
ISBN 0528 82369-8

**illustrated by John Berry**

# Illustrated Classics
# ROBINSON CRUSOE
Daniel Defoe

RAND McNALLY & COMPANY

CHICAGO · NEW YORK · SAN FRANCISCO

## My Early Life

I was born in the year 1632, in the city of York, of a good family, though not of that country, my father being a foreigner of Bremen, who settled first at Hull: he got a good estate by merchandise, and, leaving off his trade, lived afterwards at York, from whence he had married my mother, whose relations were named Robinson, a very good family in that country, and from whom I was called Robinson Kreutznaer; but, by the usual corruption of words in England, we are now called, nay, we call ourselves, and write our name, Crusoe, and so my companions always called me.

I had two elder brothers, one of which was lieutenant-colonel to an English regiment of foot in Flanders, and was killed at the battle near Dunkirk against the Spaniards: what became of my second brother I never knew, any more than my father or mother did know what was become of me.

Being the third son of the family, and not bred to any trade, my head began to be filled very early with rambling thoughts. My father had given me a competent share of learning, and designed me for the law; but I would be satisfied with nothing but going to sea, and my inclination to this led me so strongly against the will, nay, the commands of my father, and against all the entreaties and persuasions of my mother and friends, that there seemed to be something fatal in that propension of nature tending directly to the life of misery which was to befall me.

My father, a wise and grave man, gave me serious and excellent counsel against what he foresaw was my design. I was sincerely affected with this discourse, but, alas! a few days wore it all off; and, in short, to prevent any of my father's further importunities, in a few weeks after I resolved to run quite away from him.

## My First Voyage

Being one day at Hull, where I went casually, and without any purpose of making an elopement, and one of my friends being going to sea to London in his father's ship, and prompting me to go with them, I consulted neither father nor mother any more, and in an ill hour, on the 1st of September, 1651, I went on board a ship bound for London. Never any young adventurer's misfortunes, I believe, began sooner, or continued longer than mine. The ship was no sooner gotten out of the Humber but the wind began to blow, and the waves to rise in a most frightful manner. After a violent storm, our ship was wrecked off Yarmouth. I had not the sense to go back to Hull, but continued on to London, where I went on a vessel bound for the coast of Africa.

My next voyage was on a Guinea trader, and I fell into terrible misfortunes on this voyage—namely, our ship, making her course towards the Canary Islands, was surprised in the grey of the morning by a Turkish rover of Sallee, and we were all carried prisoners into Sallee, a port belonging to the Moors. I was held as a slave for several years, until I eventually made my escape on board a ship bound for the Brazils.

In Brazil I prospered, and became a successful planter and merchant for many years; however I was not content, but must go to sea again, and boarded

a ship bound for Guinea. The same day I went on board we set sail, standing away to the northward upon our own coast, with design to stretch over for the African coast. We had very good weather all the way upon our own coast, till we came to the height of Cape St. Augustino; from whence, keeping farther off at sea, we lost sight of land. Then a violent tornado or hurricane took us quite out of our knowledge. It began from the south-east, came about to the north-west, and then settled in the north-east; from whence it blew in such a terrible manner that for twelve days together we could do nothing but drive, and, scudding away before it, let it carry us whither ever fate and the fury of the winds directed.

# Shipwrecked

A second storm then came upon us, and carried us away with the same impetuosity westward, and drove us so out of the way of all human commerce, that, had our lives been saved as to the sea, we were rather in danger of being devoured by savages than ever returning to our own country.

In this distress, the wind still blowing very hard, one of our men early in the morning called out "Land!" and we had no sooner run out of the cabin to look out in hopes of seeing whereabouts in the world we were, but the ship struck upon a sand, and in a moment, her motion being so stopped, the sea broke over her in such a manner, that we expected we should all have perished immediately, and we were driven into our close quarters to shelter us from the very foam and spray of the sea.

It is not easy for anyone who has not been in the like condition to describe or conceive the consternation of men in such circumstances; we were in a dreadful condition indeed, and had nothing to do but to think of saving our lives as best we could. We had a boat on board, but how to get her off into the sea was a doubtful thing. However, there was no room for debate, for we fancied the ship would break in pieces every minute. The mate of the vessel lays hold of the boat, and with the help of the rest of the men, they got her slung over the ship's side, and, getting all into her, we let go, and committed ourselves to God's mercy and the wild sea.

And now our case was very dismal indeed, for we all saw plainly that the sea went so high, that the boat could not live, and that we should be inevitably drowned. After we had rowed, or rather driven, about a league and a half, a raging wave, mountain-like, came rolling astern of us, and plainly bade us expect the *coup-de-grâce*. In a word, it took us with such a fury, that it overset the boat at once, and we were all swallowed up in a moment.

Nothing can describe the confusion of thought which I felt when I sunk into the water; for though I swam very well, yet I could not deliver myself from the waves so as to draw breath, till that a wave, having driven me, or rather carried me, a vast way on towards the shore, and having spent itself, went back, and left me upon the land almost dry, but half-dead with the water I took in. I had so much presence of mind as well as breath left that, seeing myself nearer the mainland than I expected, I got upon my feet, and endeavoured to make on towards the land as fast as I could, before another wave should return and take me up again. But I soon found it was impossible to avoid it; for I saw the sea come after me as high as a great hill and as furious as an enemy which I had no means or strength to contend with. My business was to hold my breath and rise myself upon the water if I could, and so by swimming pilot myself towards the shore.

The wave that came upon me again buried me at once twenty or thirty feet deep in its own body; and I could feel myself carried with a mighty force and swiftness towards the shore a very great way. I was covered again with water for a good while, but I held out until it had spent itself and begun to subside. Then I struck forward against the return of the waves, and felt ground again with my feet. I stood still a few moments to recover breath, till the water went from me, and then took to my heels and ran with what strength I had farther towards the shore.

The final surge, though it broke over me, did not swallow me up, and the next run I took got me to the mainland, where I sat down upon the grass, quite out of reach of the wild sea.

# I Am Saved

I was now landed, and safe on shore, but as for my comrades, I never saw them afterwards, or any sign of them, except three of their hats, one cap, and two shoes that were not fellows.

After a while I began to look round me to see what kind of place I was in, and what was next to be done. I soon found my comforts abate, and that in a word I had a dreadful deliverance: for I was wet, had no clothes to shift me, nor anything either to eat or drink to comfort me, neither did I see any prospect before me, but that of perishing with hunger, or being devoured by wild beasts; and that which was particularly afflicting to me was that I had no weapon either to hunt and kill any creature for my sustenance, or to defend myself against any other creature that might desire to kill me for theirs. In a word, I had nothing about me but a knife, a tobacco-pipe, and a little tobacco in a box; this was all my provision, and this threw me into terrible agonies of mind, that for a while I ran about like a madman. Night coming upon me, I began with a heavy heart to consider what would be my lot if there were any ravenous beasts in that country, seeing at night they always come abroad for their prey.

All the remedy that offered to my thoughts at the time was to get up into a thick bushy tree like a fir, but thorny, which grew near me, and where I resolved to sit all night, and consider the next day what death I should die, for as yet I saw no prospect of life. I walked about a furlong from the shore, to see if I could find any fresh water to drink, which I did, to my great joy; and having drunk and put a little tobacco in my mouth to prevent hunger, I went to the tree, and getting up into it, endeavoured to place myself so as that if I should sleep I might not fall; and having cut me a short stick, like a truncheon, for my defence, I took up my lodging, and having been excessively fatigued, I fell fast asleep and slept as comfortably as, I believe, few could have done in my condition, and found myself the most refreshed with it that I think I ever was on such an occasion.

# I Visit the Wreck

When I waked it was broad day, the weather clear, and the storm abated, so that the sea did not rage and swell as before; but that which surprised me most was that the ship was lifted off in the night from the sand where she lay, by the swelling of the tide, and was driven up almost as far as the rocks; this being within about a mile from where I was, and the ship seeming to stand upright still, I wished myself on board, that, at least, I might save some necessary things for my use.

When I came down from my apartment in the tree, I looked about me again, and the first thing I found was the boat, which lay as the wind and the sea had tossed her up upon the land, about two miles on my right hand. I walked as far as I could upon the shore to have got to her, but found a neck or inlet of water between me and the boat, which was about half a mile broad, so I came back for the present, being more intent upon getting at the ship, where I hoped to find something for my present subsistence.

A little after noon I found the sea very calm, and the tide ebbed so far out that I could come within a quarter of a mile of the ship; and here I found a fresh renewing of my grief, for I saw evidently that if we had kept on board, we had been all safe, that is to say, we had all got safe on shore, and I had not been so miserable as to be left entirely destitute of all comfort and company, as I now was; this forced tears from my eyes again, but as there was little relief, I resolved, if possible, to get to the ship, so I pulled off my shirt, for the weather was hot to extremity, and took the water, but when I came to the ship, my difficulty was still greater to know how to get on board, for as she lay aground, and high out of the water, there was nothing within my reach to lay hold of. I swam round her twice, and the second time I spied a small piece of a rope, which I wondered I did not see at first, hang down by the forechains so low as that with great difficulty I got hold of it, and by the help of that rope, got up into the forecastle of the ship. My first work was to search and to see what was spoiled and what was free; and first I found that all the ship's provisions were dry and untouched by the water, and being very well disposed to eat, I went to the bread-room and filled my pockets with biscuit, and ate it as I went about other things, for I had no time to lose. I also found some rum in the great cabin, of which I took a large dram, and which I had indeed need enough of to spirit me for what was before me. Now I wanted nothing but a boat to furnish myself with many things which I foresaw would be very necessary to me.

## I Build a Raft

It was in vain to sit still and wish for what was not to be had, and this extremity roused my application. We had several spare yards, and two or three large spars of wood, and a spare top-mast or two in the ship; I resolved to fall to work with these, and I flung as many of them over board as I could manage for their weight, tying every one with a rope that they might not drive away; when this was done I went down the ship's side, and pulling them to me, I tied four of them fast together at both ends as well as I could, in the form of a raft, and laying two or three short pieces of plank upon them crossways, I found I could walk upon it very well, but that it was not able to bear any great weight, the pieces being too light; so I went to work, and with the carpenter's saw I cut a spare top-mast into three lengths, and added them to my raft, with a great deal of labour and pains; but hope of furnishing myself with necessaries encouraged me to go beyond what I should have been able to have done upon another occasion.

My raft was now strong enough to bear any reasonable weight. I first laid all the planks or boards upon it that I could get. I then got three of the seamen's chests, which I had broken open and emptied, and lowered them down upon my raft; the first of these I filled with provision, viz. bread, rice, three Dutch cheeses, five pieces of dried goat's flesh,

which we lived much upon, and a little remainder of European corn which had been laid by for some fowls which we brought to sea with us, but the fowls were killed; there had been some barley and wheat together, but, to my great disappointment, I found afterwards that the rats had eaten or spoiled it all; as for liquors, I found several cases of bottles belonging to our skipper, in which were some cordial waters, and in all about five or six gallons of rack; these I stored by themselves, there being no need to put them into the chest, nor room for them.

Next, tools to work with on shore, and it was after

long searching that I found out the carpenter's chest, which was indeed a very useful prize to me; I got it down to my raft, even whole as it was, without losing time to look into it, for I knew in general what it contained.

My next care was for some ammunition and arms; there were two very good fowling-pieces in the great cabin, and two pistols; these I secured first, with some powder-horns, and a small bag of shot, and two old rusty swords; I knew there were three barrels of powder in the ship, but knew not where our gunner had stowed them, but with much search I found

them, two of them dry and good, the third had taken water; those two I got to my raft, with the arms; and now I thought myself pretty well freighted, and began to think how I should get to shore with them, having neither sail, oar, nor rudder, and the least cap full of wind would have overset all my navigation.

I had three encouragements: first, a smooth calm sea; second, the tide rising, and setting in to the shore; third, what little wind there was blew me towards the land; and thus, having found two or three broken oars belonging to the boat, and besides the tools which were in the chest, I found two saws, an axe, and a hammer, and with this cargo I put to sea.

At length I spied a little cove on the right shore of the creek, to which with great pain and difficulty I guided my raft, and at last got so near, that, reaching ground with my oar, I could thrust her directly in; but here I had like to have dipped all my cargo in the sea again; for that shore lying pretty steep, that is to say sloping, there was no place to land but where one end of my float, if it ran on shore, would lie so high, and the other sink lower as before, that it would endanger my cargo again. All that I could do was to wait till the tide was at the highest, keeping the raft with my oar like an anchor to hold this side of it fast to the shore; near a flat piece of ground, which I expected the water would flow over; and so it did. As soon as I found water enough, for my raft drew about a foot of water, I thrust her on upon that flat piece of ground, and there fastened or moored her by sticking my two broken oars into the ground, one on one side near one end, and one on the other side near the other end; and thus I lay till the water ebbed away and left my raft and all my cargo safe on shore.

My next work was to view the country, and seek a proper place for my habitation. There was a hill not above a mile from me, which rose up very steep and high, and which seemed to over-top some other hills, which lay as in a ridge from it northward. I took out one of the fowling-pieces, and one of the pistols, and a horn of powder, and thus armed I travelled for discovery up to the top of that hill, where, after I had with great labour and difficulty got to the top, I saw that I was in an island environed every way with the sea, no land to be seen, except some rocks which lay a great way off, and two small islands less than this, which lay about three leagues to the west.

13

# My Second Voyage to the Wreck

Contented with this discovery, I came back to my raft, and fell to work to bring my cargo on shore, which took me up the rest of that day. At night, I barricaded myself round with the chests and boards I had brought on shore, and made a kind of hut for my lodging.

I now began to consider that I might yet get a great many things out of the ship, which would be useful to me, and particularly some of the rigging, and sails, and such other things as might come to land, and I resolved to make another voyage on board the vessel.

Having got my second cargo on shore, I went to work to make me a little tent with the sail and some poles which I cut for that purpose, and into this tent I brought everything that I knew would spoil, either with rain or sun, and I piled all the empty chests and casks up in a circle round the tent, to fortify it from any sudden attempt, either from man or beast.

When I had this done I blocked up the door of the tent with some boards within, and an empty chest set up on end without, and spreading one of the beds upon the ground, laying my two pistols just at my head, and my gun at length by me, I went to bed for the first time, and slept very quietly all night, for I was very weary and heavy; for the night before I had slept little, and had laboured very hard all day, as well to fetch all those things from the ship, as to get them on shore.

After this I went every day on board, and brought away what I could get.

I had now been thirteen days on shore, and had been eleven times on board the ship. But preparing the twelfth time to go on board, I found the wind begin to rise; however, at low water I went on board, and though I thought I had rummaged the cabin so effectually as that nothing more could be found, yet I discovered a chest with drawers in it, in one of which I found two or three razors, and one pair of scissors, with some ten or a dozen of good knives and forks; in another I found about thirty-six pounds' value in money, some European coin, some Brazilian, some pieces of eight, some gold, some silver. I smiled to myself at the sight of this money. "O drug!" said I aloud, "what art thou good for? Thou art not worth to me, no, not the taking off of the ground; one of those knives is worth all this

14

heap; I have no manner of use for thee, even remain where thou art, and go to the bottom as a creature whose life is not worth saving."

However, upon second thoughts, I took it away, and wrapping all this in a piece of canvas, I began to think of making another raft, but while I was preparing this, I found the sky overcast, and the wind began to rise, and in a quarter of an hour it blew a fresh gale from the shore; it presently occurred to me that it was in vain to pretend to make a raft with the wind off shore, and that it was my business to be gone before the tide of flood began, otherwise I might not be able to reach the shore at all. Accordingly I let myself down into the water, and swam across the channel which lay between the ship and the sand, and was at last gotten home to my little tent, where I lay with all my wealth about me very secure.

## My New Home

In search of a place to settle permanently, I found a little plain on the side of a rising hill, whose front towards this little plain was steep as a house-side, so that nothing could come down upon me from the top; on the side of this rock there was a hollow place worn a little way in like the entrance or door of a cave, but there was not really any cave or way into the rock at all.

On the flat of the green, just before this hollow place, I resolved to pitch my tent. This plain was not above an hundred yards broad, and about twice as long, and lay like a green before my door, and at the end of it descended irregularly every way down into the low grounds by the sea side. It was on the N.N.W. side of the hill, so that I was sheltered from the heat every day, till it came to a west and by south sun, or thereabouts, which in those countries is near the setting.

Before I set up my tent, I drew a half circle before the cave entrance which took in about ten yards in its semi-diameter from the rock, and twenty yards in its diameter, from its beginning and ending.

In this half circle I pitched two rows of strong stakes, driving them into the ground till they stood very firm like piles, the biggest end being out of the ground about five foot and a half, and sharpened on the top. The two rows did not stand above six inches from one another.

Then I took some pieces of cable which I had brought from the ship, and I laid them in rows one

upon another, within the circle, between these two rows of stakes, up to the top, placing other stakes in the inside, leaning against them, about two foot and a half high, like a spur to a post, and this fence was so strong that neither man or beast could scale it.

The entrance into this place I made by a short ladder to go over the top. Into this fence or fortress, with infinite labour, I carried all my riches, all my provisions, ammunition, and stores.

After I had been there about ten or twelve days, it came into my thoughts that I should lose my reckoning of time for want of books and pen and ink, and should even forget the sabbath days from the working days; but to prevent this I cut it with my knife upon a large post, in capital letters, and making it into a great cross I set it up on the shore where I first landed, viz. "I came on shore here on the 30th of Sept. 1659." Upon the sides of this

square post I cut every day a notch with my knife, and every seventh notch was as long again as the rest, and every first day of the month as long again as that long one, and thus I kept my calendar, or weekly, monthly, and yearly reckoning of time. And I must not forget that we had in the ship a dog and two cats, of whose eminent history I may have occasion to say something in its place; for I carried both the cats with me, and as for the dog, he jumped out of the ship of himself, and swam on shore to me the day after I went on shore with my first cargo, and was a trusty servant to me many years; I wanted nothing that he could fetch me, nor any company that he could make up to me, I only wanted to have him talk to me, but that would not do. As I observed before, I found pen, ink, and paper, and I husbanded them to the utmost, and I shall show, that while my ink lasted, I kept things very exact, but after that

was gone I could not, for I could not make any ink by any means that I could devise.

And now I began to apply myself to make such necessary things as I found I most wanted, as particularly a chair and a table; for without these I was not able to enjoy the few comforts I had in the world; I could not write, or eat, or do several things with so much pleasure without a table. So I went to work; I made abundance of things, even without tools, and some with no more tools than an adze and a hatchet. But having gotten over these things in some measure, and having settled my household stuff and habitation, made me a table and a chair, and all as handsome about me as I could, I began to keep my journal, of which I shall here give you the copy (though in it will be told all these particulars over again) as long as it lasted, for having no more ink I was forced to leave it off.

# My Journal

*September 30, 1659*

I, poor, miserable Robinson Crusoe, being shipwrecked during a dreadful storm in the offing, came on shore on this dismal unfortunate island, which I called the Island of Despair, all the rest of the ship's company being drowned, and myself almost dead.

All the rest of that day I spent in afflicting myself at the dismal circumstances I was brought to, viz. I had neither food, house, clothes, weapon, nor place to fly to, and in despair of any relief, saw nothing but death before me, either that I should be devoured by wild beasts, murdered by savages, or starved to death for want of food. At the approach of night, I slept in a tree for fear of wild creatures, but slept soundly though it rained all night.

*October 1*

In the morning I saw to my great surprise the ship had floated with the high tide, and was driven on shore again much nearer the island. I went upon the sand as near as I could, and then swam on board; this day also it continued raining, though with no wind at all.

*From the 1st October to the 24th*

All these days entirely spent in many several voyages to get all I could out of the ship.

*Oct. 20*

I overset my raft and all the goods I had got upon it, but being in shoal water, and the things being chiefly heavy, I recovered many of them when the tide was out.

*Oct. 25*

It rained all night and all day, with some gusts of wind, during which time the ship broke in pieces.

*Oct. 26*

I walked about the shore almost all day to find out a place to fix my habitation, greatly concerned to secure myself from an attack in the night, either from wild beasts or men. Towards night, I fixed upon a proper place under a rock, and marked out my encampment, which I resolved to strengthen with a wall.

*From the 26th to the 30th*

I worked very hard in carrying all my goods to my new habitation, though some part of the time it rained exceeding hard.

*The 31st*

In the morning I went out into the island with my gun to see for some food, and discover the country, when I killed a she-goat, and her kid followed me home, which I afterwards killed also because it would not feed.

*November 1*

I set up my tent under a rock, and lay there for the first night, making it as large as I could with stakes driven in to swing my hammock upon.

*Nov. 2*

I set up all my chests and boards, and the pieces of timber which made my rafts, and with them formed a fence round me, a little within the place I had marked out for my fortification.

*Nov. 3*

I went out with my gun and killed two fowls like ducks, which were very good food. In the afternoon went to work to make me a table.

*Nov. 4*

This morning I began to order my times of work, of going out with my gun, time of sleep, and time of diversion.

*Nov. 5*

This day went abroad with my gun and my dog, and killed a wild cat.

*Nov. 6*

After my morning walk I went to work with my table again, and finished it, though not to my liking; nor was it long before I learned to mend it.

*Nov. 7*

Now it began to be settled fair weather. The 7th, 8th, 9th, 10th, and part of the 12th (for the 11th was Sunday) I took wholly up to make me a chair.

*Nov. 13*

This day it rained, which refreshed me exceedingly, and cooled the earth, but it was accompanied with terrible thunder and lightning, which frighted me dreadfully for fear of my powder.

*Nov. 14, 15, 16*

These three days I spent in making little square chests or boxes, which might hold a pound or two pound, at most, of powder, and so putting the powder in, I stowed it in places as secure and remote from one another as possible. On one of these three days I killed a large bird that was good to eat, but I know not what to call it.

*Nov. 17*

This day I began to dig behind my tent into the rock to make room for my farther conveniency. Note: Three things I wanted exceedingly for this work, viz. a pick-axe, a shovel, and a wheel-barrow or basket; so I desisted from my work, and began to consider how to supply that want and make me some tools; as for a pick-axe, I made use of the iron crows, which were proper enough, though heavy; but the next thing was a shovel or spade; this was so absolutely necessary, that indeed I could do nothing effectually without it, but what kind of one to make I knew not.

*Nov. 18*

The next day in searching the woods I found a tree of that wood, or like it, which in the Brazils they call the iron tree, for its exceeding hardness; of this, with great labour and almost spoiling my axe, I cut a piece, and brought it home too with difficulty enough, for it was exceedingly heavy.

The excessive hardness of the wood, and having no other way, made me a long while upon this machine, for I worked it effectually by little and little into the form of a shovel or spade, the handle exactly shaped like ours in England, only that the broad part having no iron shod upon it at bottom, it would not last me so long; however, it served well enough for the uses which I had occasion to put it to; but never was a shovel, I believe, made after that fashion, or so long a making.

I was still deficient, for I wanted a basket or a wheel-barrow; a basket I could not make by any means, having no such things as twigs that would bend to make wicker ware, at least none yet found out; and as to a wheel-barrow, I fancied I could make all but the wheel, but that I had no notion of, neither did I know how to go about it; besides, I had no possible way to make the iron gudgeons for the spindle or axis of the wheel to run in, so I gave it over, and so for carrying away the earth which I dug out of the cave, I made me a thing like a hod, which the labourers carry mortar in when they serve the bricklayers.

This was not so difficult to me as the making the shovel; and yet this, and the shovel, and the attempt which I made in vain to make a wheel-barrow, took me up no less than four days; I mean, always excepting my morning walk with my gun, which I seldom failed, and very seldom failed also bringing home something fit to eat.

*Nov. 23*

My other work having now stood still, because of my making these tools, when they were finished I went on, and working every day, as my strength and time allowed, I spent eighteen days entirely in widening and deepening my cave, that it might hold my goods commodiously.

*Note:*

During all this time, I worked to make this room or cave spacious enough to accommodate me as a warehouse or magazine, a kitchen, a dining-room, and a cellar; as for my lodging, I kept to the tent, except that sometimes in the wet season of the year, it rained so hard that I could not keep myself dry, which caused me afterwards to cover all my place within my pale with long poles in the form of rafters leaning against the rock, and load them with flags and large leaves of trees like a thatch.

# A Lucky Escape

*December 10*

I began now to think my cave or vault finished, when on a sudden (it seems I had made it too large) a great quantity of earth fell down from the top and one side, so much that in short it frightened me, and not without reason too; for I had had a lucky escape. Upon this disaster I had great deal of work to do over again; for I had the loose earth to carry out, and which was of more importance, I had the ceiling to prop up, so that I might be sure no more would come down.

*Dec. 11*

This day I went to work with it accordingly, and got two shores or posts pitched upright to the top, with two pieces of boards across over each post; this I finished the next day; and setting more posts up with boards, in about a week more I had the roof secured, and the posts, standing in rows, served me for partitions to part of my house.

*Dec. 17*

From this day to the twentieth I placed shelves, and knocked up nails on the posts to hang everything

up that could be hung up, and now I began to be in some order within doors.

*Dec. 20*

Now I carried everything into the cave, and began to furnish my house, and set up some pieces of boards, like a dresser, to order my victuals upon, but boards began to be very scarce with me; also I made me another table.

*Dec. 24*

Much rain all night and all day; no stirring out.

*Dec. 25*

Rain all day.

*Dec. 26*

No rain, and the earth much cooler than before, and pleasanter.

*Dec. 27*

Killed a young goat, and lamed another so that I caught it, and led it home in a string; when I had it home, I bound and splintered up its leg, which was broken. N.B. I took such care of it that it lived, and the leg grew well, and as strong as ever; but by my nursing it so long it grew tame, and fed upon the little green at my door, and would not go away. This was the first time that I entertained a thought of breeding up some tame creatures, that I might have food when my powder and shot was all spent.

*Dec. 28, 29, 30*

Great heats and no breeze; so that there was no stirring abroad, except in the evening for food; this time I spent in putting all my things in order within doors.

*January 1*

Very hot still, but I went abroad early and late with my gun, and lay still in the middle of the day. This evening, going farther into the valleys which lay towards the centre of the island, I found there was plenty of goats, though exceeding shy and hard to come at; however I resolved to try if I could not bring my dog to hunt them down.

*Jan. 2*

Accordingly, the next day I went out with my dog, and set him upon the goats; but I was mistaken, for they all faced about upon the dog, and he knew his danger too well, for he would not come near them.

*Jan. 3*

I began my fence or wall; which, being still jealous of my being attacked by somebody, I resolved to make very thick and strong.

All this time I worked very hard on my wall, and made my rounds in the woods every day.

# Exploring the Island

It was the 15th of July that I began to take a more particular survey of the island itself. I went up the creek first, where, as I hinted, I brought my rafts on shore. I found, after I came about two miles up, that the tide did not flow any higher, and that it was no more than a little brook of running water, and very fresh and good; but this being the dry season, there was hardly any water in some parts of it, at least not enough to run in any stream so as it could be perceived.

I spent all that evening there, and went not back to my habitation, which, by the way, was the first night, as I might say, I had lain from home. In the night I took my first contrivance, and got up into a tree, where I slept well, and the next morning proceeded upon my discovery, travelling nearly four miles, as I might judge by the length of the valley, keeping still due north, with a ridge of hills on the south and northside of me.

At the end of this march I came to an opening, where the country seemed to descend to the west, and a little spring of fresh water, which issued out of the side of the hill by me, ran the other way, that is, due east; and the country appeared so fresh, so green, so flourishing, everything being in a constant verdure or flourish of spring, that it looked like a planted garden.

I descended a little on the side of that delicious vale, surveying it with a secret kind of pleasure (though mixed with my other afflicting thoughts)—to think that this was all my own, that I was king and lord of all this country indefeasibly, and had a right of possession; and if I could convey it, I might have it in inheritance as completely as any lord of a manor in England. I saw here abundance of cocoa trees, orange, and lemon, and citron trees; but all wild, and very few bearing any fruit, at least not then. However, the green limes that I gathered were not only pleasant to eat, but very wholesome; and I mixed their juice afterwards with water, which made it very wholesome, and very cool and refreshing. I found melons on the ground in great abundance, and grapes upon the trees.

I found now I had business enough to gather and carry home; and I resolved to lay up a store, as well of grapes as limes and lemons, to furnish myself for the wet season, which I knew was approaching. Having spent three days on this journey, I then returned home; for so I must now call my cave.

24

# My First Boat

Two more seasons passed, then, one day, travelling about my island, I came within view of the sea to the west, and it being a very clear day I fairly descried land; whether an island or continent I could not tell.

This at length put me upon thinking whether it was not possible to make myself a canoe, or periagua, such as the natives of those climates make, even without tools, or, as I might say, without hands, viz. of the trunk of a great tree. I was so intent upon my voyage over the sea in it, that I never once considered how I should get it off the land; and it was really in its own nature more easy for me to guide it over forty five miles of sea, than about forty fathoms of land, where it lay, to set it afloat in the water.

I went to work upon this boat the most like a fool that ever man did, who had any of his senses awake. I pleased myself with the design, without determining whether I was ever able to undertake it; not but that the difficulty of launching my boat came often into my head; but I put a stop to my own enquiries into it, by this foolish answer which I gave myself, "Let's first make it, I'll warrant I'll find some way or other to get it along when 'tis done."

This was a most preposterous method; but the eagerness of my fancy prevailed, and to work I went. I felled a cedar tree: I question much whether Solomon ever had such a one for the building of the temple of Jerusalem. It was five foot ten inches diameter at the end of twenty two foot, after which it lessened for a while, and then parted into branches. It was not without infinite labour that I felled this tree; I was twenty days hacking and hewing at it at the bottom; I was fourteen more getting the branches and limbs and the vast spreading head of it cut off, which I hacked and hewed through with axe and hatchet, and inexpressible labour; after this, it cost me a month to shape it, and dub it to a proportion, and to something like the bottom of a boat, that it might swim upright as it ought to do. It cost me near three months more to clear the inside, and work it out so as to make an exact boat of it. This I did indeed without fire, by mere mallet and chisel, and by the dint of hard labour, till I had brought it to be a very handsome periagua, and big enough to have carried me and all my cargo.

When I had gone through this work, I was extremely delighted with it. The boat was really

much bigger than I ever saw a canoe that was made of one tree, in my life. Many a weary stroke it had cost, you may be sure; and there remained nothing but to get it into the water; and had I gotten it into the water, I make no question but I should have begun the maddest voyage, and the most unlikely to be performed, that ever was undertaken.

But all my devices to get it into the water failed me; though they cost me infinite labour too. This grieved me heartily, and now I saw, though too late, the folly of beginning a work before we count the cost, and before we judge rightly of our own strength to go through with it.

## Making an Umbrella

I saved the skins of all the creatures that I killed, I mean four-footed ones, and I had hung them up stretched out with sticks in the sun, by which means some of them were so dry and hard that they were fit for little, but others, it seems, were very useful. The first thing I made of these was a great cap for my head, with the hair on the outside to shoot off the rain; and this I performed so well, that after this I made me a suit of clothes wholly of these skins, that is to say, a waistcoat, and breeches open at knees, and both loose, for they were rather wanting to keep me cool than to keep me warm. I must not omit to acknowledge that they were wretchedly made; for if I was a bad carpenter, I was a worse tailor. However, they were such as I made good shift with; and when I was abroad, if it happened to rain, the hair of my waistcoat and cap being outermost, I was kept very dry.

After this I spent a great deal of time and pains to make me an umbrella; I was indeed in great want of one, and had a great mind to make one; I had seen them made in Brazil, where they are very useful in the great heats which are there; and I felt the heats every jot as great here, and greater too, being nearer the equinox; besides, as I was obliged to be much abroad, it was a most useful thing to me, as well for the rains as the heats. I took a world of pains at it, and was a great while before I could make anything likely to hold; nay, after I thought I had hit the way, I spoiled two or three before I made one to my mind; but at last I made one that answered indifferently well. The main difficulty I found was to make it to let down. I could make it to spread, but if it did not let down too, and draw in, it was not portable for me any way but just over my head, which would not do. However, at last, as I said, I made one to answer, and covered it with skins, the hair upwards, so that it cast off the rains like a penthouse, and kept off the sun so effectually, that I could walk out in the hottest of the weather with greater advantage than I could before in the coolest, and when I had no need of it, could close it and carry it under my arm.

# My "Family"

Being now in the eleventh year of my residence, I set myself to study some art to trap and snare the wild goats that roamed the island, to see whether I could not catch some of them alive. To this purpose, I made snares to hamper them, and at length resolved to try a pit-fall, in which I trapped three kids. In about a year and a half I had a flock of about twelve goats, and in two years more I had three and forty. Now I not only had goats flesh to feed on when I pleased, but milk too, sometimes a gallon or two in a day.

It would have made a Stoic smile to have seen me and my little family sit down to dinner, and to see how like a king I dined, too, all alone, attended by my servants. Poll, the young parrot I had caught and tamed, was the only person permitted to talk to me, like a favourite. My dog—who was now grown very old and crazy—sat always at my right hand; and two cats, the descendants of those I had brought on shore, one on one side the table and one on the other, expecting now and then a bit from my hand, as a mark of special favour.

Had anyone in England been to meet such a man as I was, it must either have frighted them, or raised a great deal of laughter. Be pleased to take a sketch of my figure as follows.

I had my great, high shapeless cap, made of a goat's skin, with a flap hanging down behind, as well to keep the sun from me as to shoot the rain off from running into my neck. I had a short jacket of goatskin, the skirts coming down to about the middle of my thighs; and a pair of open-kneed breeches of the same—the breeches were made of the skin of an old he-goat, whose hair hung down such a length on either side, that like pantaloons it reached to the middle of my legs; stockings and shoes I had none, but had made me a pair of somethings, I scarce know what to call them, but they were of a most barbarous shape— as indeed were the rest of my clothes.

I had on a broad belt of goatskin dried, and in a kind of a frog on either side of this, instead of a sword and dagger hung a little saw and hatchet. I had another belt not so broad, which hung over my shoulder; and at the end of it hung two pouches, both made of goat's skin too—in one of which hung my powder, in the other my shot. I carried my gun on my shoulder; and over my head a great clumsy, ugly, goatskin umbrella—but which, after all, was the most necessary thing I had about me, next to my gun.

As for my face, the colour of it was not really so Mulatto-like as one might expect. My beard I had once suffered to grow until it hung about a quarter of a yard long, but as I had both scissors and razors sufficient, I had cut it pretty short, except what grew on my upper lip, which I had trimmed into a large pair of whiskers, of a length and shape monstrous enough, and such as in England would have passed for frightful.

During this time I built another canoe, which I fitted with mast and sail, and used for short voyages on the sea, but I never ventured far from my little creek.

# A Mysterious Footprint

It happened one day about noon going towards my boat, I was exceedingly surprised with the print of a man's naked foot on the shore, which was very plain to be seen in the sand. I stood like one thunderstruck, or as if I had seen an apparition; I listened, I looked round me, I could hear nothing, nor see anything; I went up to a rising ground to look farther; I went up the shore and down the shore, but it was all one, I could see no other impression but that one.

I slept none that night; the farther I was from the occasion of my fright, the greater my apprehensions were, which is something contrary to the nature of such things, and especially to the usual practice of all creatures in fear: but I was so embarrassed with my own frightful ideas of the thing, that I formed nothing but dismal imaginations to myself, even though I was now a great way off it. Some times I fancied it must be the devil; and reason joined in with me upon this supposition; for how should any other thing in human shape come into the place? Where was the vessel that brought them? What marks were there of any other footsteps? And how was it possible a man should come there?

Now I began to take courage, and to peep abroad again, for I had not stirred out of my castle for three days and nights, so that I began to starve for provision; for I had little or nothing within doors but some barley cakes and water. Then I knew that my goats wanted to be milked too, which usually was my evening diversion; and the poor creatures were in great pain and inconvenience for want of it; and indeed, it almost spoiled some of them, and almost dried up their milk.

For several years, I went about the whole island, then, one day, when wandering more to the west point of the island than I had ever gone yet, and looking out to sea, I thought I saw a boat upon the sea, at a great distance; I had found a perspective glass or two in one of the seamen's chests, which I saved out of our ship; but I had it not about me, and this was so remote that I could not tell what to make of it, though I looked at it till my eyes were not able to hold to look any longer. Whether it was a boat or not, I do not know; but as I descended from the hill, I could see no more of it, so I gave it over; only I resolved to go no more out without a perspective glass in my pocket.

When I was come down the hill to the end of the

bones of human bodies; and particularly I observed a place where there had been a fire made, and a circle dug in the earth, like a cockpit, where it is supposed the savage wretches had sat down to their inhuman feastings upon the bodies of their fellow creatures.

I was so astonished with the sight of these things, that I entertained no notions of any danger to myself from it for a long while; all my apprehensions were buried in the thoughts of such a pitch of inhuman, hellish brutality, and the horror of the degeneracy of human nature. I could not bear to stay in the place a moment longer so I got me up the hill again with all the speed I could, and walked on towards my own habitation.

Thus the years passed, and I began to be very well contented with the life I led, if it might but have been secured from the dread of the savages.

But it was otherwise directed; and it may not be amiss for all people who shall meet with my story, to make this just observation from it, namely, how frequently, in the course of our lives, the evil which in itself we seek most to shun and which when we are fallen into it is the most dreadful to us, is often times the very means or door of our deliverance, by which alone we can be raised again from the affliction we are fallen into.

## A Cannibal Feast

It was now the month of December, in my twenty-third year; and this being the southern solstice, for winter I cannot call it, was the particular time of my harvest, and required my being pretty much abroad in the fields; when going out pretty early in the morning, even before it was thorough day-light, I was surprised with seeing a light of some fire upon the shore, at a distance from me of about two miles towards the end of the island, where I had observed some savages had been as before; but not on the other side; but to my great affliction, it was on my side of the island.

I was indeed terribly surprised at the sight, and stopped short within my grove, not daring to go out, lest I might be surprised; and yet I had no more peace within, from the apprehensions I had that if these savages, in rambling over the island, should find my corn standing or cut, or any of my works and improvements, they would immediately conclude that there were people in the place, and would

island, where indeed I had never been before, I was presently convinced that the seeing the print of a man's foot was not such a strange thing in the islands as I imagined; and but that it was a special providence that I was cast upon the side of the island where the savages never came, I should easily have known that nothing was more frequent than for the canoes from the main, when they happened to be a little too far out at sea, to shoot over to that side of the island for harbour; likewise as they often met and fought in their canoes, the victors, having taken any prisoners, would bring them over to this shore, where according to their dreadful customs, being all cannibals, they would kill and eat them; of which hereafter.

When I was come down the hill to the shore, as I said above, being the S.W. point of the island, I was perfectly confounded and amazed; nor is it possible for me to express the horror of my mind, at seeing the shore spread with skulls, hands, feet, and other

then never give over till they had found me out. In this extremity I went back directly to my castle, pulled up the ladder after me, and made all things without look as wild and natural as I could.

Then I prepared myself within, putting myself in a posture of defence; I loaded all my cannon, as I called them, that is to say, my muskets which were mounted upon my new fortification, and all my pistols, and resolved to defend myself to the last gasp, not forgetting seriously to commend myself to the divine protection, and earnestly to pray to God to deliver me out of the hands of the barbarians; and in this posture I continued about two hours; but began to be mighty impatient for intelligence abroad, for I had no spies to send out.

After sitting a while, and musing what I should do, I was not able to bear sitting in ignorance any longer; so setting up my ladder to the side of the hill, I mounted to the top. Pulling out my perspective glass, which I had taken on purpose, I laid me down flat on my belly on the ground, and began to look for the place; I presently found there was no less than nine naked savages, sitting round a small fire they had made, not to warm them, for they had no need of that, the weather being extremely hot; but, as I supposed, to dress some of their barbarous diet of human flesh, which they had brought with them, whether alive or dead I could not know.

They had two canoes with them, which they had hauled up upon the shore; and as it was then tide of ebb, they seemed to me to wait for the return of the flood, to go away again; it is not easy to imagine what confusion this sight put me into, especially seeing them come on my side the island, and so near me too; but when I observed their coming must always be with the current of the ebb, I began afterwards to be more sedate in my mind, being satisfied that I might go abroad with safety all the time of the tide of flood, if they were not on shore before: and having made this observation, I went abroad about my harvest work with the more composure.

As I expected, as soon as the tide made to the westward, I saw them all take the boat, and row (or paddle as we call it) all away. I should have observed, that for an hour and more before they went off, they went to dancing, and I could easily discern their postures and gestures by my glasses: I could not perceive, by my nicest observation, but that they were stark naked, and had not the least

34

covering upon them; but whether they were men or women, that I could not distinguish.

As soon as I saw them shipped and gone, I took two guns upon my shoulders, and two pistols at my girdle, and my great sword by my side, without a scabbard, and with all the speed I was able to make, I went away to the hill, where I had discovered the first appearance of all; and as soon as I got thither, which was not less than two hours (for I could not go apace, being so loaded with arms as I was), I perceived there had been three canoes more of savages on that place; and looking out farther, I saw they were all at sea together, making over for the main.

This was a dreadful sight to me, especially when going down to the shore, I could see the marks of horror which the dismal work they had been about had left behind it, viz. the blood, the bones, and part of the flesh of human bodies, eaten and devoured by those wretches, with merriment and sport. I was so filled with indignation at the sight, that I began now to premeditate the destruction of the next that I saw there, let them be who or how many soever.

## I Rescue a Savage

Two more years passed, then I was surprised one morning early, with seeing no less than five canoes all on shore together on my side the island; and the people who belonged to them all landed and out of my sight. The number of them broke all my measures, for seeing so many, and knowing that they always came four or six, or sometimes more in a boat, I could not tell what to think of it, or how to take my measures to attack twenty or thirty men single handed; so I lay still in my castle, perplexed and discomforted; however, I put myself into all the same postures for an attack that I had formerly provided, and was just ready for action, if anything had presented. Having waited a good while, listening to hear if they made any noise, at length, being very impatient, I set my guns at the foot of my ladder, and clambered up to the top of the hill; standing so, however, that my head did not appear above the hill, so that they could not perceive me by any means; here I observed, by the help of my perspective glass, that they were no less than thirty in number, they

had a fire kindled, and they had meat dressed. How they had cooked it, that I knew not, or what it was; but they were all dancing in I know not how many barbarous gestures and figures, their own way round the fire.

While I was thus looking on them, I perceived by my perspective two miserable wretches dragged from the boats, where it seems they were laid by, and were now brought out for the slaughter: I perceived one of them immediately fell, being knocked down, I suppose with a club or wooden sword, for that was their way, and two or three others were at work immediately cutting him open for their cookery, while the other victim was left standing by himself, till they should be ready for him. In that very moment this poor wretch seeing himself a little at liberty, nature inspired him with hopes of life, and he started away from them, and ran with incredible swiftness along the sands directly towards me, I mean that part of the coast where my habitation was.

I was dreadfully frightened when I perceived him to run my way, and especially when, as I thought, I saw him pursued by the whole body. However, I kept my station, and my spirits began to recover when I found that there were not above three men that followed him, and still more was I encouraged when I found that he outstripped them exceedingly in running, and gained ground on them, so that if he could but hold it for half an hour, I saw easily he would fairly get away from them all.

There was between them and my castle the creek; and this, I saw plainly, he must necessarily swim over, or the poor wretch would be taken there. But when the savage escaping came thither, he made nothing of it, though the tide was then up, but plunging in, swam through in about thirty strokes or thereabouts, landed, and ran on with exceeding strength and swiftness; when the three persons came to the creek, I found that two of them could swim, but the third could not, and that standing on the other side, he looked at the others, but went no further, and soon after went softly back again, which, as it happened, was very well for him in the main.

I observed that the two who swam were yet more

37

than twice as long swimming over the creek as the fellow was that fled from them. It came now very warmly upon my thoughts, and indeed irresistibly, that now was my time to get me a servant, and perhaps a companion or assistant; and that I was called plainly by providence to save the poor creature's life, I fetched my two guns, and getting up again with the same haste to the top of the hill, I crossed towards the sea; and making a short cut, nearly all downhill, placed myself between pursuers and pursued. I shouted to him that fled, and beckoned for him to come back. I then turned to the two who followed. The first I knocked down with the stock of my piece, the second, while he was raising his bow and arrow, I killed with my first shot.

The poor savage who fled had now stopped and though he saw his enemies lying dead, was so fearful that he stood stock still, and made no effort to come forward. I smiled and made signs to him to advance. At length he did so, then kneeling down placed his face upon the ground. He then took my foot and placed it upon his head, thus displaying that he was my slave forever.

## My Man Friday

I took him up and made much of him, and encouraged him all I could. I gave him bread and raisins to eat, and a draught of water. And, having refreshed him, I made signs for him to lie down and sleep, which he did straight away.

He was a comely, handsome fellow, perfectly well made, with straight strong limbs, not too large, tall and well shaped, and about twenty-six years of age. He had a very good countenance, especially when he smiled. His hair was long and black, his forehead very high and large, and a great vivacity and sparkling sharpness in his eyes. The colour of his skin was not quite black, but very tawny.

After he had slumbered, I made him know his name should be Friday, which was the day I saved his life. I likewise taught him that my name was to be Master and taught him to say it, and Yes and No, and to know the meaning of them.

The night came and we slept. In the morning I beckoned him to come with me. I gave him the sword, bows and arrows, and one of the guns to carry, and we marched away to the place these creatures had been.

When we arrived there, my blood chilled in my

veins, for all variety of human remnants littered the ground; skulls, bones, flesh and blood covered half eaten morsels. In short, evidence of a wild cannibal feast. Friday conveyed to me that they had brought over four prisoners to feast upon. Three had been eaten, and he was to be the fourth.

I told Friday to gather all the remains and burn them. When this had been done we returned to my castle. There I kitted out my savage. I gave him a pair of linen drawers which I had out of the poor gunner's chest I mentioned, and which I found in the wreck; and which with a little alteration fitted him very well.

Never man had a more faithful, loving, sincere servant, than Friday was to me; without passions, sullenness, or designs, perfectly obliged and engaged; his very affections were tied to me, like those of a child to a father; and I dare say he would have sacrificed his life for the saving mine upon any occasion whatsoever. The many testimonies he gave me of this put it out of doubt, and soon convinced me that I needed to use no precautions as to my safety on his account.

I was greatly delighted with him, and made it my business to teach him everything that was proper to make him useful, handy, and helpful; but especially to make him speak, and understand me when I spake; and he was the aptest scholar that ever was, and particularly was so merry, so constantly diligent, and so pleased, when he could but understand me, or make me understand him, that it was very pleasant to talk to him.

This was the pleasantest year of all the life that I led in this place. Friday began to talk pretty well, and understand the names of almost everything I had occasion to call for, and of every place I had to send him to, and to talk a great deal to me. Besides the pleasure of talking to him, I had a singular satisfaction in the fellow himself. His simple, unfeigned honesty appeared to me more and more every day.

He told me that up a great way beyond the moon, that was, beyond the setting of the moon, which must be W. from their country, there dwelt white men, like me; and that they had killed "much mans", that was his word. By all which I understood, he meant the Spaniards, whose cruelties in America had been spread over the whole country, and was remembered by all the nations from father to son.

I enquired if he could tell me how I might come from this island, and get among those white men; he told me, "yes, yes", I might go "in two canoe"; I could not understand what he meant, or make him describe to me what he meant by "two canoe", till at last, with great difficulty, I found he meant it must be in a large great boat, as big as two canoes.

This part of Friday's discourse began to relish with me very well, and from this time I entertained some hopes, that one time or other, I might find an opportunity to make my escape from this place; and that this poor savage might be a means to help me to do it.

After Friday and I became more intimately acquainted, and that he could understand almost all I said to him and speak fluently, though in broken English, to me, I acquainted him with my own story, or at least so much of it is as related to my coming into the place, how I had lived there, and how long. I let him into the mystery, for such it was to him, of gunpowder and bullet, and taught him how to shoot; I gave him a knife, which he was wonderfully delighted with, and I made him a belt, with a frog hanging to it, such as in England we wear hangers in; and in the frog, instead of a hanger, I gave him a hatchet, which was not only as good a weapon in some cases, but much more useful upon other occasions.

## Preparing for a Voyage

I showed him the ruins of our boat, which we lost when we were wrecked, and which I could not stir with my whole strength then, but was now fallen almost to pieces. Upon seeing this boat, Friday stood musing a great while, and said nothing. I asked him what it was he studied upon; at last said he, "Me see such boat like come to place at my nation."

I did not understand him a good while; but at last, when I had examined farther into it, I understood by him that a boat, such as that had been, came on shore upon the country where he lived; that is, as he explained it, was driven thither by stress of weather. I presently imagined that some European ship must have been cast away upon their coast, and the boat might get loose, and drive ashore; but was so dull, that I never once thought of men making escape from a wreck thither, much less whence they might come; so I only inquired after a description of the boat.

Friday described the boat to me well enough; but brought me better to understand him, when he added with some warmth, "We save the white mans from drown." Then I presently asked him if there was any white mans, as he called them, in the boat. 'Yes,' he said, "the boat full white mans." I asked him how many; he told upon his fingers seventeen. I asked him then what became of them; he told me, "They live, they dwell at my nation."

From this time I confess I had a mind to venture over, and see if I could possibly join with these men, who I had no doubt were Spaniards or Portuguese;

not doubting but if I could, we might find some method to escape from thence, being upon the continent, and a good company together; better than I could from an island forty miles off the shore, and alone without help. So after some days I took Friday to work again, by way of discourse, and told him I would give him a boat to go back to his own nation; and accordingly I carried him to my frigate which lay on the other side of the island, and having cleared it of water, for I always kept it sunk in the water, I brought it out, showed it him, and we both went into it.

I found he was a most dexterous fellow at managing it, he would make it go almost as swift and fast again as I could; so when he was in, I said to him, "Well now, Friday, shall we go to your nation?" He looked very dull at my saying so, which it seems was because he thought the boat too small to go so far.

Upon the whole, I was by this time so fixed upon my design of going over with him to the continent, that I told him we would go and make one as big as required and he should go home in it. There were trees enough in the island to have built a little fleet, not of periaguas and canoes, but even of good large vessels. But the main thing I looked at, was to get one so near the water that we might launch it when it was made, to avoid the mistake I committed at first.

At last, Friday pitched upon a tree, for I found he knew much better than I what kind of wood was fittest for it, nor can I tell to this day what wood to call the tree we cut down, except that it was very like the tree we call fustic, or between that and the Nicaragua wood, for it was much the same colour and smell. Friday was for burning the hollow or cavity of the tree out to make it for a boat. But I showed him how rather to cut it out with tools, which, after I had showed him how to use, he did very handily, and in about a month's hard labour we finished it, and made it very handsome, especially when with our axes, which I showed him how to handle, we cut and hewed the outside into the true shape of a boat; after this, however, it cost us near a fortnight's time to get her along as it were inch by inch upon great rollers into the water. But when she was in, she would have carried twenty men with great ease.

I had a farther design, and that was to make a mast and sail and to fit her with an anchor and cable. As to a mast, that was easy enough to get; so I pitched upon a straight young cedar-tree, which I found near the place, and which there was great plenty of in the island, and I set Friday to work to cut it down, and gave him directions how to shape and order it. I was preparing daily for the voyage; and the first thing I did was to lay by a certain quantity of provisions, being the stores for our voyage; and intended, in a week or a fortnight's time, to open the dock and launch our boat.

## More Cannibals

I was busy one morning upon some thing of this kind, when I called to Friday, and bade him go to the sea shore, and see if he could find a turtle or tortoise, a thing which we generally got once a week, for the sake of the eggs as well as the flesh. Friday had not been long gone, when he came running back, and flew over my outer wall, or fence, like one that felt not the ground, or the steps he set his feet on; and

before I had time to speak to him, he cried out to me, "O master; O master! O sorrow! O bad!" "What's the matter, Friday?" said I. "O yonder, there," said he, "one, two, three canoe! One, two, three!" By his way of speaking, I concluded there were six; but on inquiry, I found it was but three. "Well, Friday," said I, "do not be frightened"; so I heartened him up as well as I could. However, I saw the poor fellow was most terribly scared.

I entered the wood, with all possible wariness and silence, Friday following close at my heels. I marched till I came to the skirt of the wood, on the side which was next to them; only that one corner of the wood lay between me and them; here I called softly to Friday, and showing him a great tree, which was just at the corner of the wood, I bade him go to the tree, and bring me word if he could see there plainly what they were doing. He did so, and came immediately back to me, and told me they might be plainly viewed there; that they were all about their fire, eating the flesh of one of their prisoners; and that another lay bound upon the sand, a little from them, which he said they would kill next, and which fired all the very soul within me; he told me it was not one of their nation, but one of the bearded men, who he had told me of, that came to their country in the boat. I was filled with horror at the very naming of the white bearded man, and going to the tree, I saw plainly by my glass a white man who lay upon the beach of the sea, with his hands and his feet tied, with flags, or things like rushes; and that he was a European, and had clothes on.

## We Rescue a Spaniard

There was another tree, and a little thicket beyond it, about fifty yards nearer to them than the place where I was, which by going a little way about, I saw I might come at undiscovered, and that then I should be within half shot of them; so I withheld my passion, though I was indeed enraged to the highest degree, and going back about twenty paces, I got behind some bushes, which held all the way till I came to the other tree; and then I came to a little rising ground, which gave me a full view of them, at the distance of about eighty yards.

I had not a moment to lose; for nineteen of the dreadful wretches sat upon the ground, all close

huddled together, and had just sent the other two to butcher the poor Christian, and bring him, perhaps limb by limb to their fire, and they were stooped down to untie the bands at his feet; I turned to Friday. "Now, Friday," said I, "do as I bid thee;" Friday said he would. "Then, Friday," said I, "do exactly as you see me do, fail in nothing." So I set down one of the muskets and the fowling-piece upon the ground, and Friday did the like by his; and with the other musket I took my aim at the savages, bidding him do the like. Then asking him if he was ready, he said "Yes." "Then fire at them," said I; and the same moment I fired also.

Friday took his aim so much better than I, that on the side that he shot, he killed two of them and wounded three more; and on my side, I killed one, and wounded two. They were, you may be sure, in a dreadful consternation; and all of them who were not hurt, jumped up upon their feet, but did not immediately know which way to run, or which way to look; for they knew not from whence their destruction came. Friday kept his eyes close upon me, that, as I had bid him, he might observe what I did. So as soon as the first shot was made, I threw down the piece and took up the fowling-piece, and Friday did the like; he saw me cock and present; he did the same again. "Are you ready, Friday?" said I. "Yes," said he. "Let fly then," said I, "in the name of God," and with that I fired again among the amazed wretches, and so did Friday; and as our pieces were now loaded with what I called swan-shot, or small pistol bullets, we found only two drop; but so many were wounded, that they ran about yelling and screaming like mad creatures, all bloody and miserably wounded, most of them; whereof three more fell quickly after, though not quite dead.

"Now, Friday," said I, laying down the discharged pieces, and taking up the musket which was yet loaded, "follow me," which he did, with a great deal of courage. Upon which I rushed out of the wood, and showed myself, and Friday close at my foot. As soon as I perceived they saw me, I shouted as loud as I could, and bade Friday do so too; and running as fast as I could, which by the way, was not very fast, being loaded with arms as I was, I made directly towards the poor victim, who was, as I said, lying upon the beach or shore, between the place where they sat and the sea. The two butchers who were just going to work with him had left him at the surprise of our first fire, and fled in a terrible fright to the

48

seaside and had jumped into a canoe, and three more of the rest made the same way. I turned to Friday, and bade him step forwards and fire at them. He understood me immediately, and running about forty yards to be near them, he shot at them, and I thought he had killed them all; for I saw them fall of a heap into the boat; though I saw two of them up again quickly. However, he killed two of them and wounded the third; so that he lay down in the bottom of the boat, as if he had been dead.

While my man Friday fired at them, I pulled out my knife and cut the flags that bound the poor victim, and loosing his hands and feet, I lifted him up, and asked him in the Portuguese tongue what he

was. He answered in Latin, "Christianus"; but was so weak and faint that he could scarce stand or speak. I took my bottle out of my pocket and gave it him, making signs that he should drink, which he did; and I gave him a piece of bread, which he ate. Then I asked him what countryman he was, and he said, "Espagniole"; and being a little recovered, let me know by all the signs he could possibly make, how much he was in my debt for his deliverance. "Seignior," said I, with as much Spanish as I could make up, "we will talk afterwards, but we must fight now. If you have any strength left, take this pistol and sword, and lay about you." He took them very thankfully, and no sooner had he the arms in his

hands, but, as if they had put new vigour into him, he flew upon his murderers like a fury, and had cut two of them in pieces in an instant. For the truth is, as the whole was a surprise to them, so the poor creatures were so much frighted with the noise of our pieces, that they fell down for mere amazement and fear; and had no more power to attempt their own escape, than their flesh had to resist our shot. And that was the case of those five that Friday shot at in the boat; for as three of them fell with the hurt they received, so the other two fell with the fright.

I kept my piece in my hand still, without firing, being willing to keep my charge ready, because I had given the Spaniard my pistol and sword; so I called to Friday, and bade him run up to the tree from whence we first fired, and fetch the arms which lay there, which he did with great swiftness; and then giving him my musket, I sat down myself to load all the rest again, and bade them come to me when they wanted. While I was loading these pieces, there happened a fierce engagement between the Spaniard and one of the savages, who made at him with one of their great wooden swords, the same weapon that

was to have killed him before, if I had not prevented it. The Spaniard, who was as bold and as brave as could be imagined, though weak, had fought this Indian a good while, and had cut him two great wounds on his head; but the savage being a stout lusty fellow, closing in with him, had thrown him down (being faint) and was wringing my sword out of his hand, when the Spaniard, though undermost, wisely quitting the sword, drew the pistol from his girdle, shot the savage through the body, and killed him upon the spot, before I, who was running to help him, could come near him.

Friday, being now left to his liberty, pursued the flying wretches with no weapon in his hand but his hatchet; and with that he dispatched those three who, as I said before, were wounded at first and fallen, and all the rest he could come up with; and the Spaniard coming to me for a gun, I gave him one of the fowling-pieces, with which he pursued two of the savages, and wounded them both; but as he was not able to run, they both got from him into the wood, where Friday pursued them and killed one of them; but the other was too nimble for him, and though he was wounded, yet had plunged himself into the sea, and swam with all his might off to those two who were left in the canoe, which three in the canoe, with one wounded, who we know not whether he died or no, were all that escaped our hands of one and twenty.

My thoughts were a little suspended when I had a serious discourse with the Spaniard, and when I understood that there were sixteen more of his countrymen and Portuguese, who having been cast away, and made their escape to that side, lived there at peace indeed with the savages, but were very sore put to it for necessaries and indeed for life.

He told me they were all of them very civil, honest men, and they were under the greatest distress imaginable, having neither weapons nor clothes, nor any food, but at the mercy and discretion of the savages; out of all hopes of ever returning to their own country; and that he was sure, if I would undertake their relief, they would live and die by me.

Having prepared a larger stock of food for all the guests I expected, I gave the Spaniard leave to go over to the main, to see what he could do with those he had left behind him there. I gave him a strict charge in writing not to bring any man with him who would not first swear that he would in no way injure, fight with, or attack the person he should find in the island.

# A Ship Approaches

It was no less than eight days I had waited for them, when a strange and unforeseen accident intervened. I was fast asleep in my hutch one morning, when my man Friday came running in to me, and called aloud, "Master, master, they are come, they are come!"

I jumped up, and regardless of danger, I went out, as soon as I could get my clothes on, through my little grove, which by the way was by this time grown to be a very thick wood. I say, regardless of danger, I went without my arms, which was not my custom

to do; but I was surprised, when turning my eyes to the sea, I presently saw a boat at about a league and a half's distance, standing in for the shore, with a shoulder of mutton sail, as they call it; and the wind blowing pretty fair to bring them in; also I observed presently that they did not come from that side which the shore lay on, but from the southernmost end of the island. Upon this I called Friday in, and bade him lie close, for these were not the people we looked for, and that we might not know yet whether they were friends or enemies.

Having fetched my perspective glass, and climbed

the ladder, I had scarce set my foot on the hill when my eye plainly discovered a ship lying at anchor, at about two leagues and a half's distance from me south-south-east, but not above a league and a half from the shore. By my observation it appeared plainly to be an English ship, and the boat appeared to be an English long-boat.

I cannot express the confusion I was in, though the joy of seeing a ship, and one who I had reason to believe was manned by my own countrymen, and consequently friends, was such as I cannot describe; but yet I had some secret doubts hung about me, I cannot tell from whence they came, bidding me keep upon my guard.

In the first place, it occurred to me to consider what business an English ship could have in that part of the world, since it was not the way to or from any part of the world where the English had any traffic; and I knew there had been no storms to drive them in there. It was most probable that they were here upon no good design.

I saw the boat draw near the shore, as if they looked for a creek to thrust in at for the convenience of landing; however, as they did not come quite far enough, they did not see the little inlet where I formerly landed my rafts; but ran their boat on shore upon the beach, at about half a mile from me, which was very happy for me; for otherwise they would have landed just, as I may say, at my door, and would soon have beaten me out of my castle, and perhaps have plundered me of all I had. When they were on shore, I was fully satisfied that they were Englishmen; at least most of them. One or two I thought were Dutch, but it did not prove so.

# Mutiny

There were in all eleven men, whereof three of them I found were unarmed, and, as I thought, bound; and when the first four or five of them were jumped on shore, they took those three out of the boat as prisoners. One of the three I could perceive using passionate gestures of entreaty, affliction, and despair, even to a kind of extravagance; the other two I could perceive lifted up their hands sometimes, and appeared concerned indeed, but not to such a degree as the first.

I was perfectly confounded at the sight, and knew not what the meaning of it should be. Friday called out to me in English, as well as he could. "O master! you see English mans eat prisoner as well as savage mans." "Why," said I, "Friday, do you think they are a-going to eat them then?" "Yes," said Friday, "they will eat them." "No, no, Friday, I am afraid they will murder them indeed, but you may be sure they will not eat them."

All this while I had no thought of what the matter really was, but stood trembling with the horror of the sight, expecting every moment when the three prisoners should be killed; nay, once I saw one of the villains lift up his arm with a great cutlass, to strike one of the poor men; and I expected to see him fall every moment, at which all the blood in my body seemed to run chill in my veins.

After I had observed the outrageous usage of the three men by the insolent seamen, I observed the fellows run scattering about the land, as if they wanted to see the country. I observed that the three other men had liberty to go also where they pleased; but they sat down all three upon the ground, very pensive, and looked like men in despair.

This put me in mind of the first time when I came on shore, and began to look about me; how I gave myself over for lost; how wildly I looked round me; what dreadful apprehensions I had; and how I lodged in the tree all night for fear of being devoured by wild beasts.

As I knew nothing that night of the supply I was to receive by the providential driving of the ship nearer the land, by the storms and tide, by which I have since been so long nourished and supported; so these three poor desolate men knew nothing how certain of deliverance and supply they were, how near it was to them, and how effectually and really they were in a condition of safety, at the same time that they thought themselves lost, and their case desperate.

It was just at the top of high-water when these people came on shore, and while partly they stood parleying with the prisoners they brought, and partly while they rambled about to see what kind of a place they were in, they had carelessly stayed till the tide was spent and the water was ebbed considerably away, leaving their boat aground.

They had left two men in the boat, who, as I found afterwards, having drank a little too much brandy, fell asleep; however, one of them waking sooner than the other, and finding the boat too fast aground for him to stir it, hallooed for the rest who were straggling about, upon which they all soon came to the boat; but it was past all their strength to launch her, the boat being very heavy, and the shore on that side being a soft oozy sand, almost like a quick-sand.

In this condition, like true seamen who are perhaps the least of all mankind given to fore-thought, they gave it over, and away they strolled about the country again; and I heard one of them say aloud to another, calling them off from the boat, "Why, let her alone, Jack, can't ye, she will float next tide," by which I was fully confirmed in the main enquiry, of what countrymen they were.

I knew it was no less than ten hours before the boat could be afloat again, and by that time it would be dark, and I might be at more liberty to see their motions, and to hear their discourse, if they had any. In the meantime, I fitted myself up for a battle, as before, though with more caution, knowing I had to do with another kind of enemy than I had at first. I ordered Friday also, who I had made an excellent marksman with his gun, to load himself with arms. I took myself two fowling-pieces, and I gave him three muskets. My figure indeed was very fierce; I had my formidable goat-skin coat on, with the great cap I have mentioned, a naked sword by my side, two pistols in my belt, and a gun upon each shoulder.

## The English Captain

It was my design, as I said above, not to have made any attempt till it was dark; but about two o'clock, being the heat of the day, I found that in short they were all gone straggling into the woods, and, as I thought, were laid down to sleep. The three poor distressed men, too anxious for their condition to get any sleep, were however sat down under the shelter of a great tree, at about a quarter of a mile from me, and, as I thought, out of sight of any of the rest.

Upon this I resolved to discover myself to them, and learn something of their condition. Immediately

I marched in the figure as above, my man Friday at a good distance behind me, as formidable for his arms, as I, but not making quite so staring a spectre-like figure as I did.

I came as near them undiscovered as I could and then, before any of them saw me, I called aloud to them in Spanish, "What are ye, gentlemen?"

They started up at the noise, but were ten times more confounded when they saw me, and the uncouth figure that I made. They made no answer at all, but I thought I perceived them just going to fly from me, when I spoke to them in English.

"Gentlemen," said I, "do not be surprised at me; perhaps you may have a friend near you when you did not expect it." "He must be sent directly from heaven then," said one of them gravely to me, and pulling off his hat at the same time to me, "for our condition is past the help of man." "All help is from heaven, sir," said I. "But can you put a stranger in the way how to help you, for you seem to me to be in some great distress? I saw you when you landed, and when you seemed to make applications to the brutes that came with you, I saw one of them lift up his sword to kill you."

The poor man, with tears running down his face, and trembling, looked like one astonished, returned, "Am I talking to God or man?" "I am an Englishman and disposed to assist you," I said. "I have one servant only; we have arms and ammunition; tell us freely, can we serve you? What is your case?"

"Our case," said he, 'sir, is too long to tell you, while our murderers are so near; but in short, sir, I was commander of that ship; my men have mutinied against me; they have been hardly prevailed upon not to murder me, and at last have set me on shore in this desolate place, with these two men with me, one my mate, the other a passenger, where we expected to perish, believing the place to be uninhabited, and know not yet what to think of it."

"Have they any fire-arms?" said I. He answered they had only two pieces, and one which they left in the boat. "Well then," said I, "leave the rest to me; I see they are all asleep, it is an easy thing to kill them all; but shall we rather take them prisoners?" He told me there were two desperate villains among them, that it was scarce safe to show any mercy to; but if they were secured, he believed all the rest would return to their duty. I asked him which they were. He told me he could not at that distance describe them; but he would obey my orders in anything I would direct. "Well," said I, "let us retreat out of their view or hearing, lest they awake, and we will resolve further"; so they willingly went back with me, till the woods covered us from them.

"Now," said I, "here are three muskets for you, with powder and ball; tell me next what you think is proper to be done." He showed me all the testimony of his gratitude that he was able; but offered to be wholly guided by me. I told him I thought it was hard venturing anything; but the best method I could think of was to fire upon them at once, as they lay; and if any was not killed at the first volley, and offered to submit, we might save them, and so put it wholly upon God's providence to direct the shot.

He said very modestly, that he was loth to kill them, if he could help it, but that those two were incorrigible villains, and had been the authors of all the mutiny in the ship, and if they escaped, we should be undone still; for they would go on board and bring the whole ship's company, and destroy us all. "Well then," says I, "necessity legitimates my advice, for it is the only way to save our lives." However, seeing him still cautious of shedding blood, I told him they should go themselves, and manage as they found convenient.

## We Make Our Plans

In the middle of this discourse, we heard some of them awake, and soon after we saw two of them on their feet. I asked him if either of them were of the men who he had said were the heads of the mutiny. He said, "No." "Well then," said I, "you may let them escape, and Providence seems to have wakened them on purpose to save themselves. Now," says I, "if the rest escape you, it is your fault."

Animated with this, he took the musket I had given him in his hand and a pistol in his belt, and his two comrades with him, with each man a piece in his hand. The two men who were with him, going first, made some noise, at which one of the seamen who was awake turned about, and seeing them coming, cried out to the rest; but it was too late then; for the moment he cried out, they fired—I mean the two men, the captain wisely reserving his own piece.

They had so well aimed their shot at the men they knew, that one of them was killed on the spot, and the other very much wounded; but not being dead, he started up upon his feet, and called eagerly for help to the other; but the captain, stepping to him, told him, 'twas too late to cry for help, he should call upon God to forgive his villainy, and with that word knocked him down with the stock of his musket, so that he never spoke more. There were three more in the company, and one of them was also slightly wounded. By this time I was come, and when they saw their danger, and that it was in vain to resist, they begged for mercy. The captain told them he would spare their lives, if they would give him an assurance of their abhorrence of the treachery they had been guilty of, and would swear to be faithful to him in recovering the ship, and afterwards in carrying her back to Jamaica, from whence they came. They gave him all the protestations of their sincerity that could be desired, and he was willing to believe them, and spare their lives, which I was not against; only I obliged him to keep them bound hand and foot while they were upon the island.

While this was doing, I sent Friday with the captain's mate to the boat, with orders to secure her and bring away the oars and sail, which they did; and by and by, three straggling men that were (happily for them) parted from the rest, came back upon hearing the guns fired, and seeing their captain, who before was their prisoner, now their conqueror, they submitted to be bound also; and so our victory was complete. Our business now was to consider how to recover the ship.

He agreed with me as to that, but told me he was perfectly at a loss what measures to take; for that there were still six and twenty hands on board, who having entered into a cursed conspiracy, by which they had all forfeited their lives to the law, would be hardened in it now by desperation; and would carry it on, knowing that if they were reduced, they should be brought to the gallows as soon as they came to England, or to any of the English colonies; and that therefore there would be no attacking them with so small a number as we were.

I mused for some time upon what he had said, and found it was a very rational conclusion; and that therefore some thing was to be resolved on very speedily, as well to draw the men on board into some snare for their surprise, as to prevent their landing upon us, and destroying us. Upon this it presently

occurred to me that in a little while the ship's crew, wondering what was become of their comrades and of the boat, would certainly come on shore in their other boat to seek for them, and that then perhaps they might come armed, and be too strong for us. This he allowed was rational.

Upon this, I told him the first thing we had to do was to stave the boat which lay upon the beach, so that they might not carry her off; and taking everything out of her, leave her so far useless as not to be fit to swim. Accordingly we went on board, took the arms which were left on board out of her, and whatever else we found there, which was a bottle of brandy and another of rum, a few biscuit cakes, a horn of powder, and a great lump of sugar in a piece of canvas; the sugar was five or six pounds; all which was very welcome to me, especially the brandy and sugar, of which I had had none left for many years.

We knocked a great hole in her bottom, so that if they had come strong enough to master us, yet they could not carry off the boat. Indeed, it was not much in my thoughts that we could be able to recover the ship; but my view was that if they went away without the boat, I did not much question to make her fit again, to carry us away to the Leeward Islands, and call upon our friends, the Spaniards, in my way, for I had them still in my thoughts.

While we were thus preparing our designs, and had first by main strength heaved the boat up upon the beach, so high that the tide would not float her

off at high-water-mark, we heard the ship fire a gun, and saw her make a waft with her antient, as a signal for the boat to come on board; but no boat stirred; and they fired several times, making other signals for the boat. At last, when all their signals and firing proved fruitless, and they found the boat did not stir, we saw them, by the help of my glasses, hoist another boat out, and row towards the shore; and we found as they approached that there were no less than ten men in her, and that they had fire-arms with them.

As the ship lay almost two leagues from the shore,

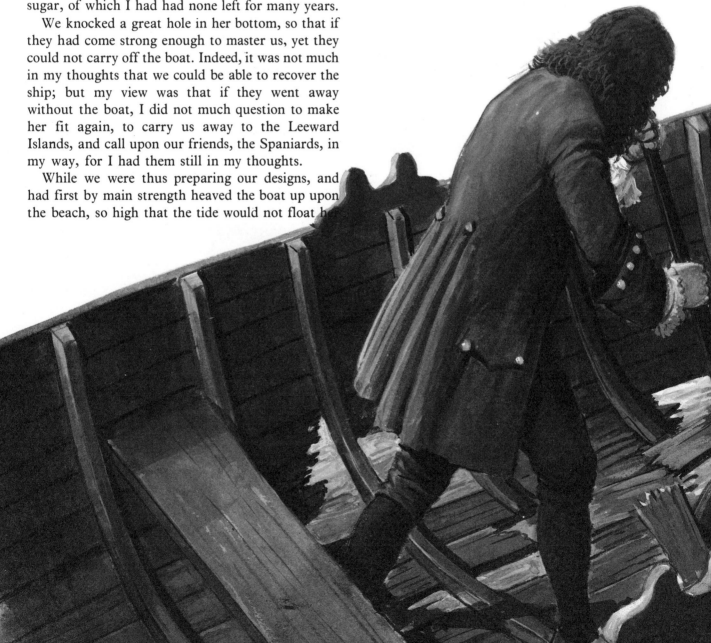

we had a full view of them as they came, and a plain sight of the men, even of their faces, because the tide having set them a little to the east of the other boat, they rowed up under shore, to come to the same place where the other had landed, and where the boat lay.

The captain knew the persons and characters of all the men in the boat, of whom he said that there were three very honest fellows, but that as for the boatswain, who it seems was the chief officer among them and all the rest, they were as outrageous as any of the ship's crew.

We had, upon the first appearance of the boat's coming from the ship, considered of separating our prisoners, and had indeed secured them effectually.

Two of them, of whom the captain was less assured than ordinary, I sent with Friday and one of the three (delivered men) to my cave, and he stood sentinel over them at the entrance. The other prisoners had better usage; two of them were kept pinioned indeed, because the captain was not free to trust them; but the other two were taken into my service upon their captain's recommendation, and upon their solemnly engaging to live and die with us;

so with them and the three honest men, we were seven men, well armed; and I made no doubt we should be able to deal well enough with the ten that were coming, considering that the captain had said there were three or four honest men among them also. As soon as they got to the place where their other boat lay, they run their boat in to the beach and came all on shore, hauling the boat up after them, which I was glad to see; for I was afraid they would rather have left the boat at anchor, some distance from the shore, with some hands in her to guard her; and so we should not be able to seize the boat.

Being on shore, the first thing they did, they ran all to their other boat, and it was easy to see that they were under a great surprise, to find her stripped as above, of all that was in her, and a great hole in her bottom.

After they had mused a while upon this, they set up two or three great shouts, hallooing with all their might, to try if they could make their companions hear; but all was to no purpose. Then they came all

close in a ring, and fired a volley of their small arms, which indeed we heard, and the echoes made the woods ring, but it was all one; those in the cave we were sure could not hear, and those in our keeping, though they heard it well enough, yet dared give no answer to them.

They were so astonished at the surprise of this, that as they told us afterwards, they resolved to go all on board again to their ship, and let them know that the men were all murdered, and the long-boat staved; accordingly they immediately launched their boat again, and got all of them on board.

The captain was terribly amazed and even confounded at this, believing they would go on board the ship again, and set sail, giving their comrades for lost, and so he should still lose the ship, which he was in hopes we should have recovered; but he was quickly as much frighted the other way.

They had not been long put off with the boat, but we perceived them all coming on shore again; but with this new measure in their conduct, which it seems they consulted together upon, namely to leave three men in the boat, and the rest to go on shore, and go up into the country to look for their fellows.

This was a great disappointment to us; for now we were at a loss what to do; for our seizing those seven men on shore would be of no advantage to us if we let the boat escape; because they would then row away to the ship, and then the rest of them would be sure to weigh and set sail, and so our recovering the ship would be lost.

However, we had no remedy but to wait and see what the issue of things might present. The seven men came on shore, and the three who remained in

the boat put her off to a good distance from the shore, and came to anchor to wait for them; so that it was impossible for us to come at them in the boat.

Those that came on shore kept close together, marching towards the top of the little hill under which my habitation lay; and we could see them plainly, though they could not perceive us. We could have been very glad they would have come nearer to us, so that we might have fired at them, or that they would have gone farther off, that we might have come abroad.

We waited a great while though very impatient for their removing; and were very uneasy, when after long consultations, we saw them start all up and march down towards the sea.

It seems they had such dreadful apprehensions upon them of the danger of the place, that they resolved to go on board the ship again, give their companions over for lost, and so go on with their intended voyage with the ship.

# Battle with the Mutineers

As soon as I perceived them go towards the shore, I imagined it to be as it really was, that they had given over their search, and were for going back again; and the captain, as soon as I told him my thoughts, was ready to sink at the apprehensions of it; but I presently thought of a stratagem to fetch them back again, and which answered my end to a tittle.

I ordered Friday and the captain's mate to go over the little creek westward, and bade them halloo as loud as they could, and wait till the seamen heard them; that as soon as they heard the seamen answer them, they could return it again, and then keeping out of sight, take a round, always answering when the other hallooed, to draw them as far into the island, and among the woods, as possible, and then wheel about again to me, by such ways as I directed them.

They were just going into the boat, when Friday and the mate hallooed, and they presently heard them, and answering, ran along the shore westward, towards the voice they heard, where they were presently stopped by the creek, where the water being up, they could not get over, and called for the boat to come up and set them over, as indeed I expected.

When they had set themselves over, I observed that the boat being gone up a good way into the creek, and as it were, in a harbour within the land, they took one of the three men out of her to go along with them, and left only two in the boat, having fastened her to the stump of a little tree on the shore.

This is what I wished for, and immediately leaving Friday and the captain's mate to their business, I took the rest with me, and crossing the creek out of their sight, we surprised the two men before they were aware; one of them lying on shore, and the other being in the boat. The fellow on shore was between sleeping and waking, and going to start up; the captain, who was foremost, ran in upon him and knocked him down, and then called out to him in the boat to yield, or he was a dead man.

There needed very few arguments to persuade a single man to yield, when he saw five men upon him, and his comrade knocked down; besides, this was, it seems, one of the three who were not so hearty in the mutiny as the rest of the crew, and therefore was easily persuaded, not only to yield, but afterwards to join sincerely with us.

In the meantime, Friday and the captain's mate so well managed their business with the rest, that they drew them by hallooing and answering, from one hill to another, and from one wood to another, till they not only heartily tired them, but left them where they were very sure they could not reach back to the boat before it was dark; and indeed they were heartily tired themselves also by the time they came back to us.

We had nothing now to do but to watch for them in the dark, and to fall upon them, so as to make sure work with them.

It was several hours after Friday came back to me, before they came back to their boat; and we could hear the foremost of them long before they came quite up, calling to those behind to come along, and could also hear them answer and complain how lame and tired they were, and not able to come any faster, which was very welcome news to us.

At length they came up to the boat; but 'tis impossible to express their confusion when they found the boat fast aground in the creek, the tide ebbed out, and their two men gone. We could hear them call to one another in a most lamentable manner, telling one another they were gotten into an enchanted island; that either there were inhabitants in it, and they should all be murdered, or else there were devils and spirits in it, and they should be all carried away and devoured.

They hallooed again, and called their two comrades by their names a great many times, but no answer. After some time, we could see them, by the little light there was, run about wringing their hands like men in despair; and that sometimes they would go and sit down in the boat to rest themselves, then come ashore again, and walk about again, and so over the same thing again.

My men would fain have me give them leave to fall upon them at once in the dark; but I was willing to take them at some advantage, so to spare them, and kill as few of them as I could; and especially I was unwilling to hazard the killing any of our own men, knowing the others were very well armed. I resolved to wait to see if they did not separate; and therefore to make sure of them, I drew my ambuscade nearer, and ordered Friday and the captain to creep upon their hands and feet as close to the ground as they could, that they might not be discovered, and get as near them as they could possibly, before they offered to fire.

They had not been long in that posture, but that the boatswain, who was the principal ringleader of the mutiny, and had now shown himself the most dejected and dispirited of all the rest, came walking towards them with two more of their crew; when they came nearer, the captain and Friday, starting up on their feet, let fly at them.

The boatswain was killed upon the spot, the next man was shot in the body and fell just by him, though he did not die till an hour or two after; and the third ran for it.

At the noise of the fire, I immediately advanced with my whole army, which was now eight men, namely myself generalissimo, Friday my lieutenant-general, the captain and his two men, and the three prisoners-of-war, who we had trusted with arms.

We came upon them indeed in the dark, so that they could not see our number; we bade them surrender, as the captain was standing by with fifty men ready to attack. This, of course, was a fiction as our active force numbered only eight in all. But it worked.

My army came up and seized them all, upon their boat, only I kept myself and one more out of sight, for reasons of state.

Our next work was to repair the boat, and think of seizing the ship.

Upon the captain's coming to me, I told him my project for doing this, which he liked wonderfully well, and resolved to put it in execution the next morning, but first it would be necessary to divide the prisoners.

I told him that he should go and take three of the worst of them, and send them pinioned to the cave where the others lay. This was committed to Friday and the two men who came on shore with the captain.

## Retaking the Ship

With the coming of morning the captain had no difficulty before him, but to furnish his two boats, stop the breach of one, and man them. He made his passenger captain of one, with four other men; and himself, and his mate, and five more, went in the other; and they contrived their business very well, for they came up to the ship about midnight. As soon as they came within call of the ship, he hailed them and told them they had brought off the men and the boat, but that it was a long time before they had found them, and the like; holding them in a chat till

they came to the ship's side; when the captain and the mate, entering first with their arms, immediately knocked down the second mate and carpenter with the butt-end of their muskets. Being very faithfully seconded by their men, they secured all the rest that were upon the main and quarter decks, and began to fasten the hatches to keep them down who were below, when the other boat and their men, entering at the fore chains, secured the fore-castle of the ship, and the scuttle which went down into the cook-room, making three men they found there prisoners.

When this was done, and all safe upon deck, the captain ordered the mate with three men to break into the round-house where the new rebel captain lay, and having taken the alarm, was gotten up, and with two men and a boy had gotten fire-arms in their hands; and when the mate with a crow split open the door, the new captain and his men fired boldly among them, and wounded the mate with a musket ball, which broke his arm, and wounded two more of the men but killed nobody.

The mate, calling for help, rushed however into the round-house, wounded as he was, and with his pistol shot the new captain through the head, the bullet entering at his mouth, and came out again behind one of his ears, so that he never spoke a word; upon which the rest yielded, and the ship was taken effectually, without any more lives lost.

As soon as the ship was thus secured, the captain ordered seven guns to be fired, which was the signal agreed upon with me, to give me notice of his success, which you may be sure I was very glad to hear, having sat watching upon the shore for it till near two o'clock in the morning.

# I Am Rescued at Last

Having thus heard the signal plainly, I laid me down; and it having been a day of great fatigue to me, I slept very sound, till I was something surprised with the noise of a gun; and presently starting up, I heard a man call me and presently I knew the captain's voice, when climbing up to the top of the hill, there he stood, and pointing to the ship, he embraced me in his arms. "My dear friend and deliverer," said he, "there's your ship, for she is all yours, and so are we and all that belong to her." I cast my eyes to the ship, and there she rode within little more than half a mile of the shore; for they had weighed her anchor as soon as they were masters of her; and the weather being fair, had brought her to an anchor just against the mouth of the little creek; and the tide being up, the captain had brought the pinnace in near the place where I at first landed my rafts, and so landed just at my door.

I was at first ready to sink down with surprise; for I saw my deliverance indeed visibly put into my hands, all things easy, and a large ship just ready to carry me away whither I pleased to go.

At first, for some time, I was not able to answer him one word; but as he had taken me in his arms, I held fast by him, or I should have fallen to the ground.

He perceived the surprise, and immediately pulled a bottle out of his pocket, and gave me a dram of cordial, which he had brought on purpose for me. After I had drunk it, I sat down upon the ground; and though it brought me to myself, yet it was a good while before I could speak a word to him.

We consulted what was to be done with the prisoners we had, and decided that, since we knew them to be incorrigible and refractory to the last degree, it was best to leave them on the island. I therefore let them into the story of my living there,

and put them in the way of making it easy to them. In a word, I gave them every part of my own story.

When we, my man Friday and I, took leave of this island, we carried on board for relics the great goat's-skin cap I had made, my umbrella, and my parrot; also I forgot not to take the money I formerly mentioned, which had lain by me so long useless that it was grown rusty, or tarnished, and could hardly pass for silver till it had been cleaned and polished.

And thus we left the island, the nineteenth of December as I found by the ship's account, in the year 1686, after I had been upon it eight and twenty years, two months, and nineteen days.

In this vessel, after a long voyage, we arrived in England, the eleventh of June, in the year 1687.